Lote Tree Learning
+1 832- 378-7365
hello@lotetreelearning.com
www.lotetreelearning.com

Ordering Information:
Quantity sales. Special discounts are available on quantity purchases by corporations, associations, and others. For details, contact us at the address above.

Printed in the United States of America

First Edition
Illustrations by Israa Alaa Ismail

Lote Tree
LEARNING

ANCIENTS

History Connections Book 1 Middle Grades

Parent Pages

SUMAIA B. MICHEL, DRS
SARA MAGDY

Lote Tree
LEARNING

Before you lies one of the books in the second series for the History Connections. It is called History Connections, because learning history is all about connections: connections to the past, and connections to each other. Knowing what happened in the past helps us make sense of our present. Knowing how we fit into the larger global history, helps us connect to others. Knowing our heritage gives us a place to belong. Knowledge of history even gives us a basis to determine future actions. Currently, the world has become a global community, thus making global history all the more pressing. This program focuses on teaching 21st century skills, rather than rote memorization of facts, as this teaches students important skills to function in the modern society of the future.

4 ERAS

Our History Connections series spans from the Ancients to the Modern Era. Every year students will take a chunk of this history. In the first book, students will cover from Creation to about 500 C.E. In the second book, they will cover from 500 C.E. until about 1650 C.E. The third era will cover from 1650 C.E. until the Industrial Revolution, approximately 1850 C.E. The last era, the Modern Era, will cover from 1850 C.E. until our current day.

All Eras have Islamic History integrated within global history, with more attention and time spend on important topics in the history of our Ummah. The four books in this curriculum are consecutive and follow each other, not only in chronological information but also in building skills. This series is intended for grades 5 through 8. The first book is best suited for late primary students, grade 5 and 6, with the next books covering grades 7 and 8.

IDEALS

Our unique approach to learning is summed up in the acronym IDEALS, which covers several methodologies and skills we believe should be covered in all educational programs, whether for primary students or adults. IDEALS stands for Inquiry Based Learning, Differentiated Learning, Experiential learning, Aptitude Training, Lens of Islam, and Social-Emotional Learning.

Inquiry-based Learning

Inquiry-based Learning is an approach to learning that emphasizes the student's role in the learning process. Rather than the teacher telling students what they need to know, students are encouraged to explore the material, ask questions, and share ideas.

Differentiation

Differentiation means tailoring instruction to meet individual needs. Differentiation is a framework for effective teaching that involves providing all learners a range of different avenues for understanding new information.

Experiential Learning

Experiential Learning is the process of learning through experience, and is more specifically defined as "learning through reflection on doing".

Aptitude Training

Aptitude Training determines how well-equipped students are to make good decisions and solve problems in their academic, professional and personal lives. Skills are the building blocks that allow students to apply the knowledge they acquire in an academic context to real world problems and situations.

Lens of Islam

Lens of Islam integrates Islamic knowledge into elements of the academic program in order to provide students with an Islamic lens to view the world and to create connections between the deen and the world at large. Viewing the world through an Islamic lens will increase a sense of purpose and meaning, and allows students to foster their Islamic identity and live with integrity.

Social-emotional Learning

Social-emotional Learning is the process through which students acquire and apply the skills necessary to manage emotions and social relationships. According to Goleman, social-emotional intelligence "emerges as a much stronger predictor of who will be most successful, because it is how we handle ourselves in our relationships that determines how well we do once we are in a given job".

MATERIALS

The History Connections Book 1 – Ancients program includes the following:

- History Connections Book 1: Ancients – Middle Grades
- History Connections Book 1: Ancients – Middle Grades: Parent Manual
- World Wall Map
- TreeTrunk Timeline

The program does NOT include the Usborne Internet Linked History Encyclopedia, abbreviated as UILE throughout this book. **The Usborne Internet Linked History Encyclopedia is essential for this program.** Please purchase this encyclopedia: most bookstores carry the book. In addition, the student will need the History Intersections, 2nd edition, as a resource for all Islamic topics. History Intersections is abbreviated as HI throughout this book. **The History Intersections is also essential for this program.**

We recommend using *The Super Servants Series* for some the Prophet stories, as an additional resource, but these are not mandatory. This series features 10 books, covering the most important prophets, and they are engaging and entertaining for kids to read.

ELEMENTS

In every lesson there are several elements, which are summarized in the Task Card on the first page of every weekly lesson:

WEEK: 1	CREATION		
RESEARCH:	Creation, Prophet Adam (as) Idrees (as)	**RESOURCES:**	UILE HI Super Servant Stories
SKILL:	Outlining	**PROJECT:**	Poster
MAPPING:	Creation	**TIMELINING:**	Adam (as)

Research

Learning how to read and understand a scientific text is an important life-skill. It helps create life-long and independent learners. In the Research box of the weekly Task Card, the key words are listed. Students are encouraged to find the topics in the encyclopedia themselves by using the content pages or the index pages. The keywords listed assist in finding the topics in the encyclopedia.

Resources

We have listed the resources that will be used for the week in the resources section of the weekly Task Card. UILE stands for the Usborne Internet Linked History Encyclopedia, HI stands for History Intersections, 2nd edition and the Super Servants Stories are optional.

Skill

The program covers a wide range of skills, including outlining, summarizing, note-taking and mind mapping. These skills are not only useful for the subject of history, but are life-skills to be used throughout a wide range of subjects, both academic as non-academic. The difficulty of the skills will be increased over several weeks, allowing the students to become proficient through small incremental steps.

Project

Every week, the student will create a project: sometimes this is with pen and paper and sometimes this is with an online software. The purpose of the project is to show information you have found in a visual manner. The student will practice a project for several weeks, so he/she can become really good at it. When making posters, we use Canva.com. This is a free website that allows the student to make posters and other graphics. He/she can go to the website and set up a free account.

Map

The student will make a map by tracing a Location Map and following the instructions every week. The instructions will tell the student what items should be marked and labeled on the map. The map should be made with colors and have as much details as possible. Every map should be labeled at the top with the topic of the week. The purpose of having the student trace the map is recognition of topographical landmarks and elements such as mountain ranges, rivers, deserts, seas, oceans, and cities. By physically tracing a map, the information is integrated into memory. Most Location Maps are traced more than once.

Timeline

Timelining involves the placement of information in chronological order on a visual that represents the passage of time. Most timelines are linear; starting from one point and moving in one direction. Such timelines will give a good sense of the order events are happening in, and which events happen at the same time. However, a linear timeline does not show the different topographical area things happen in at the same time. Therefore, our timeline is circular: it is shaped like a slice of a tree trunk, with the rings showing its years. We have also divided the circular timeline in 'slices', like a pizza. Every slice represents a different area of the world. When data is added to the timeline, all events happening in the same rings are happening at the same time, and going from the center to the outer ring in each slice, will show the order events happened in for that particular area.

Every week, the student will write the chronological information found and if applicable, the dates in the boxes in the resources, on the timeline in the topographical area the events took place in. Not only time matters, but also place. See instructions below on how to assemble the timeline.

World Wall Map

In order to have a sense where events on the traced map take place on a global scale, we will ask the student to locate the traced map area on the World Wall Map. The World Wall Map is a complete world map without details. See instructions below on how to assemble the World Wall Map

PROPOSED SCHEDULING

This curriculum contains 30 weeks of history lessons. We recommend teaching history twice a week, and we have divided the lessons in two days for this purpose. We do not recommend teaching this subject only once a week, as the resources will require ample time for reading and notetaking etc. For teaching history more than twice a week, we have given an example schedule below. Please plan for 45 minutes to complete the activities on each day. There may be times where this is significantly less or more, because the project might take time depending on the skill level of the student.

Proposed Schedule – Twice per week

DAY 1	DAY 2
• Read the pages in the resources (use the directions under Research) • Skill (outline, summarize or take notes, according to instructions) • Map • Timeline • (Start your project if time allows)	• Read the pages in the resources (use the directions under Research) • Skill (outline, summarize or take notes, according to instructions) • Project

Alternate Schedule – Four times per week

DAY 1	DAY 2	DAY 3	DAY 4
• Read the pages in the resources (use the directions under Research) • Skill (outline, summarize or take notes, according to instructions)	• Map • Timeline • (Start your project if time allows)	• Read the pages in the resources (use the directions under Research) • Skill (outline, summarize or take notes, according to instructions)	• Project

Before you start this program, assemble the World Wall Map and the Tree Trunk Timeline according to the instructions below.

Prepare the World Wall Map before the first lessons. Remove the pages for the World Wall Map from the Maps & Rubrics booklet, and keep them in order. Place them in front of you, image upwards, in landscape format. Cut off the right and bottom part of each page, as neatly on the line as possible, keeping them in order. Turn the pile upside down, and start with the page now on top. Place this page on a surface in front of you, to the bottom right, with the image upwards. Turn the next page over and place it to the left of the first page, overlapping the white border of the first page and aligning the image. Do the same with the next page and the fourth one: now the lower row is completed. Place the fifth page on the top of the first one, overlapping the top white border of the first page and aligning the image. Place the sixth one to the left of the fifth one, overlapping the top white border of the second page and the left white border of the fifth one, and align the image. Continue until all four rows (each four pages) are completed. Use a glue stick or white glue to stick all pages together. Assemble the Tree Trunk Timeline is a similar manner as the World wall map.

We recommend hanging the map on a wall where the student can easily see it, as this serves as a visual reminder. It is important when tracing a map, the student has an understanding what part of the World Map he/she is tracing. The student can use his/her hands to form a rectangular frame, the way photographers do, when he/she indicates the geographical area on the World Wall Map that is being discussed.

Should you prefer not to hang the posters on the wall, you can assemble them and add them to a foam poster board. Attach the World Wall Map on one side and the Tree Trunk Timeline on the other side. This way you can put the map and timeline away, and bring it out whenever you need it.

In these pages that follow, we have assembled an overview with the pages in the resources used, in case the student has troubles finding the required pages. We have also given a weekly overview of the requirements for the Skill and Project, so as a parent, you know what your child is supposed to do.

ASSESSMENT

The skills learned and the projects made are supposed to become better and better. In order for you to assess whether your child is on the right track and whether they are progressing, we have added check-lists and rubrics that will allow you to assess your child's work. A check-list simply lists the elements that should be present in the student's work. A rubric lists the elements to be assessed in scales of evaluation. When you see your child's work, you can find the scale your child's ability is at and see where he/she needs to work on.

The rubrics and check-lists are not intended to make the child feel bad about their work. Rather, they are intended to show their progress. At first, not all elements in a skill or projects are discussed, so when evaluating the skills or projects at first, some elements may not be present. However, by time the student's work should show progress and increase. When certain elements have been discussed and should be present but are lacking, simply discuss what is missing and encourage the student to work a bit more on these aspects. There is no problem working on a project a bit more after it has become clear something is missing.

The research questions are not represented in a rubric, as the ability to use these questions as a guideline when reading scientific text will directly show in the quality of the skills.

CONTENT

PARENT PAGES

WEEK: 1	CREATION		
RESEARCH:	Creation, Prophet Adam (as) Idrees (as)	**RESOURCES:**	HI Super Servant Stories
SKILL:	Outlining	**PROJECT:**	Poster
MAPPING:	Creation	**TIMELINING:**	Adam (as)

SKILL:

Outline the Story of Adam (as) in a basic outline. For every paragraph, write down one main point, listed with roman numerals.

PROJECT:

Have a go at making a poster yourself! Log in to canva, and choose the poster templates. Pick a design you like for the topic of this week. What design fits the story of Adam (as) well?

What would be a great title for this poster? Can you include a sub-title?

Requirements of poster: A premade poster template. Replace the title with your own. Add a subtitle. Delete information on the poster you do not need. The graphic or image of the poster has to fit the theme of the Story of Adam (as). Colors can be adjusted.

WEEK: 2	FIRST SETTLEMENTS		
KEYWORDS:	From Hunting to Farming, First Farmers	RESOURCES:	UILE
SKILL:	Outlining	PROJECT:	Poster
MAPPING:	Fertile Crescent	TIMELINING:	First Settlements

SKILL:

Outline the topic of this week. For every paragraph, write down one main point, listed with roman numerals.

PROJECT:

Which graphics would go really well with this topic? Explore the different images and elements on Canva. Pick the graphics that fit the topic for this week well.

Requirements: Pick a pre-made template based upon the parts of the poster needed. Add/remove parts as necessary. Title and subtitle should be correct. Image/graphics should match the topic.

WEEK: 3	FERTILE CRESCENT & STORY OF NUH (AS)		
KEYWORDS:	Fertile Crescent, Mesopotamia, First Towns, Prophet Nuh (as)	RESOURCES:	UILE HI Super Servants Stories
SKILL:	Outlining	PROJECT:	Poster
MAPPING:	Map of Prophet Nuh (as)	TIMELINING:	Prophet Nuh (as)

SKILL:

Outline the topic of this week. For every paragraph, write down one main point, listed with roman numerals.

PROJECT:

Which graphics would go really well with this topic?
Explore the different images and elements on Canva. Under 'photos' you will find images and under 'elements' you can find all kinds of things needed, like shapes, lines, drawn images, art etc.
Pick the graphics that fit the topic for this week well.

Requirements: Pick a pre-made template based upon the parts of the poster needed. Add/remove parts as necessary. Title and subtitle should be correct. Image/graphics should match the topic.

WEEK: 4	SUMERIANS & AKKADIANS		
KEYWORDS:	Sumer, Akkad, First Cities, Mesopotamia, Ziggurat, Crafts & Trade, Kings & Wars	RESOURCES:	UILE
SKILL:	Outlining	PROJECT:	Poster
MAPPING:	Mesopotamia	TIMELINING:	Sumer & Akkad

SKILL:

Outline the topic of this week. For every paragraph, write down one main point, listed with roman numerals.

PROJECT:

Make a poster for the topic of this week, and pay special attention to **whitespace**: where is whitespace important in your poster? Make several versions with different whitespace areas and see which one you like.

Requirements: Pick a pre-made template based upon the parts of the poster needed. Add/remove parts as necessary. Title and subtitle should be correct. Image/graphics should match the topic. Whitespace should be used correctly: a minimum of three versions with different whitespace usage are made.

WEEK: 5 **PROPHET HUD (AS) & SALEH (AS)**

KEYWORDS:	Prophet Hud (as), Prophet Saleh (as)	**RESOURCES:**	HI
SKILL:	Outlining	**PROJECT:**	Poster
MAPPING:	Prophet Hud (as) & Saleh (as)	**TIMELINING:**	Prophet Hud (as) & Saleh (as)

SKILL:

Outline the topic of this week. For every paragraph, write down one main point, listed with roman numerals.

PROJECT:

The Stories of Hud & Saleh (as) have many different elements. Pick one event of one of the stories that you liked very much and represent this in your poster. This week, pay special attention to color. Look at the colors in your image/ graphic used, and match or complement them. Change the colors in your template. Create three different versions with different colors. Which one works best with the topic of the story?

Requirements: Pick a pre-made template based upon the parts of the poster needed. Add/remove parts as necessary. Title and subtitle should be correct. Image/graphics should match the topic. Whitespace should be used correctly. Colors should be changed: a minimum of three versions with different colors.

WEEK: 6	**PROPHET IBRAHIM (AS) & LUT (AS)**		
KEYWORDS:	Prophet Ibrahim (as), Prophet Ismail (as), Prophet Ishaq (as), Prophet Lut (as) Nimrod, Mekka	**RESOURCES:**	HI Super Servant Series
SKILL:	Outlining	**PROJECT:**	Diagramming
MAPPING:	Map of Prophet Ibrahim (as)	**TIMELINING:**	Prophet Ibrahim (as), Prophet Ismail (as)

SKILL:

Outline the topic of this week. For every paragraph, write down one main point, listed with roman numerals. By now, you might think outlining is easy, so add the second level to your outlining this week.

PROJECT:

Prophet Ibrahim (as) tried in many different ways to convince his people to remember Allah (swt). Additionally, Allah (swt) also showed them a miracle.

This week, diagram all the times when Ibrahim (as) tried to convince his people, and they could have used their minds and believed in Allah (swt).

Use the the image on the previous page to choose a diagram and use the 5 steps above to guide you in making your diagram.

WEEK: 7	NILE VALLEY		
KEYWORDS:	Nile, Flooding, Upper Egypt. Lower Egypt	RESOURCES:	UILE
SKILL:	Outlining	PROJECT:	Diagramming
MAPPING:	Map of Nile Delta	TIMELINING:	Egypt

SKILL:

Outline the topic of this week. For every paragraph, write down one main point, listed with roman numerals. By now, you might think outlining is easy, so add the second level to your outlining this week.

PROJECT:

For this week, make a diagram showing the cycle of the Nile, that determined the lives of the ancient Egyptians.

Use the the image on the other page to choose a diagram and use the 5 steps above to guide you in making your diagram.

WEEK: 8   **EGYPT'S KINGDOMS**

KEYWORDS: Old, Middle and New   **RESOURCES:**   UILE
Kingdom, Mummies,
Pyramids

SKILL: Note Taking   **PROJECT:**   Diagramming

MAPPING: Pyramids of Egypt   **TIMELINING:**   Old, Middle and New
Kingdom

SKILL:

As you read, write down important terms and key words. Leave space next to the terms to add definitions later, if you cannot do so right away. Remember to use your own words!

PROJECT:

For this week, make a diagram showing the steps of making a mummy, according to the ancient Egyptians.

Use the the image on the other page to choose a diagram and use the 5 steps above to guide you in making your diagram.

WEEK: 9	**INDUS VALLEY**		
KEYWORDS:	Indus river, Mohenjo-daro, Harappa	**RESOURCES:**	UILE
SKILL:	Note Taking	**PROJECT:**	Diagramming
MAPPING:	Indus Valley	**TIMELINING:**	Indus Valley

SKILL:

As you read, write down important terms and key words. Leave space next to the terms to add definitions later, if you cannot do so right away.
Remember to use your own words!

PROJECT:

For this week, make a diagram showing all the possible reasons why the people of the Indus Valley left their city. See if you can come up with some other reasons why they may have left their cities, and add these to your diagram.

Use the the image on the other page to choose a diagram and use 5 steps above to guide you in making your diagram.

WEEK: 10	PROPHET YA'QUB (AS) & PROPHET YUSUF (AS)		
KEYWORDS:	Prophet Ya'ub (as), Prophet Yusuf (as), Egypt	**RESOURCES:**	HI Super Servant Series
SKILL:	Note Taking	**PROJECT:**	Diagramming
MAPPING:	Map of prophet Yusuf (as)	**TIMELINING:**	Prophet Yusuf (as)

SKILL:

As you read, write down important terms and key words. Leave space next to the terms to add definitions later, if you cannot do so right away.

Use at least one list of bullets or numbers in your notes today.

Remember to use your own words!

PROJECT:

For this week, make a diagram showing the lineage of Prophet Ibrahim (as) down to Yusuf (as).

Use the the image on the other page to choose a diagram and use 5 steps above to guide you in making your diagram.

WEEK: 11	STONEHENGE & MINOANS		
KEYWORDS:	Stonehenge, King Minos, Knossos, Minotaur	RESOURCES:	UILE
SKILL:	Note taking	PROJECT:	Diagramming
MAPPING:	No map this week	TIMELINING:	Stonehenge & Minoans

SKILL:

terms to add definitions later, if you cannot do so right away.

Use at least one list of bullets or numbers in your notes today.

PROJECT:

Diagram the events of the story The Legend of the Minotaur. Show step by step what happened.

Use the the image on the this page to choose a diagram and use 5 steps above to guide you in making your diagram.

WEEK: 12	**MYCENEANS**		
KEYWORDS:	Myceneans, Troy	**RESOURCES:**	UILE
SKILL:	Note Taking	**PROJECT:**	PowerPoint
MAPPING:	Greece	**TIMELINING:**	Mycenea

SKILL:

As you read, write down important terms and key words. Leave space next to the terms to add definitions later, if you cannot do so right away.
Use bullet lists and number lists when useful. Come up with at least one abbreviations in your notes today.
Remember to use your own words!

PROJECT:

You have already researched your topic for this week, so write a quick outline about the main events. Think of a catchy title and a topic sentence.
Create a PPT with a minimum of **5 slides:** one introduction slide, 3 main point slides (one main point per slide) and one conclusion slide.
The design can be simply a colored background: we will pay more attention to the design in later weeks.

WEEK: 13	PROPHET AYYUB (AS) & DHUL KIFL (AS)		
KEYWORDS:	Prophet Ayyub (as), Dhul Kifl (as)	RESOURCES:	HI Super Servants Series
SKILL:	Note Taking	PROJECT:	PowerPoint
MAPPING:	Prophet Ayyub (as), Dhul Kifl (as)	TIMELINING:	Prophet Ayyub (as), Dhul Kifl (as)

SKILL:

As you read, write down important terms and key words. Leave space next to the terms to add definitions later, if you cannot do so right away.
Use bullet lists and number lists when useful. Come up with at least *two more* abbreviations in your notes today.
Remember to use your own words!

PROJECT:

You have already researched your topic for this week, so write a quick outline about the main events. Think of a catchy title and a topic sentence.

Pick a template to use for your presentation this week.

Create a PPT with a minimum of 5 slides: one introduction slide, 3 main point slides (one main point per slide) and one conclusion slide.

WEEK: 14	HAMMURABI & THE HITTITES		
KEYWORDS:	Hammurabi's Law, Babylonian Empire, Hittites	**RESOURCES:**	UILE
SKILL:	Note Taking	**PROJECT:**	PowerPoint
MAPPING:	Babylonian Empire & the Hittite Empire	**TIMELINING:**	Babylonian Empire & the Hittite Empire

SKILL:

As you read, write down important terms and key words. Leave space next to the terms to add definitions later, if you cannot do so right away.

Use bullet lists and number lists when useful. Come up with at least *three more* abbreviations in your notes today.

Remember to use your own words!

PROJECT:

You have already researched your topic for this week, so write a quick outline about the main events. Think of a catchy title and a topic sentence.

Pick a template to use for your presentation this week.

Add at least one image or clip art to your presentation that supports the main point.

Create a PPT with a minimum of 5 slides: one introduction slide, 3 main point slides (one main point per slide) and one conclusion slide.

WEEK: 15	**PEOPLE OF CANAAN**		
KEYWORDS:	Canaanites, Sea People, Philistines	**RESOURCES:**	UILE
SKILL:	Summarizing	**PROJECT:**	PowerPoint
MAPPING:	Canaan	**TIMELINING:**	People of Canaan

SKILL:

This week, we will focus on step 1 & 2. Read the text for the day, without making any notes (step 1).
Once you have read it, ask yourself: what is this text trying to tell me?
Write down some of the main ideas in one or two sentences.

PROJECT:

You have already researched your topic for this week, so write a quick outline about the main events. Think of a catchy title and a topic sentence.
Pick a template to use for your presentation this week.
Add at least one image or clip art to your presentation that supports the main point.
Create a PPT with a minimum of 7 slides: one introduction slide, 5 main point slides (one main point per slide) and one conclusion slide.

WEEK: 16	PROPHET SHU'AYB (AS), PROPHET MUSA (AS) & THE ISRAELITES		
KEYWORDS:	Prophet Musa (as), Prophet Shu'ayb (as), Israel, Hebrews, Jews	RESOURCES:	UILE HI Super Servants Series
SKILL:	Summarizing	PROJECT:	PowerPoint
MAPPING:	Prophet Musa (as) Prophet Shu'ayb (as)	TIMELINING:	Prophet Musa (as) Prophet Shu'ayb (as)

SKILL:

This week, we will focus on step 1 & 2. Read the text (step 1), and think about the main points of the text (step 2).
Write down some of the main ideas in one or two sentences.

PROJECT:

You have already researched your topic for this week, so write a quick outline about the main events. Think of a catchy title and a topic sentence.
Pick a template to use for your presentation this week.
Add at least one image or clip art to your presentation that supports the main point.
Create a PPT with a minimum of 7 slides: one introduction slide, 5 main point slides (one main point per slide) and one conclusion slide.

WEEK: 17	**PROPHET DAWUD (AS) & PROPHET SULAYMAN (AS)**		
KEYWORDS:	Prophet Dawud (as), Prophet Sulayman (as)	RESOURCES:	HI Super Servants Series
SKILL:	Summarizing	PROJECT:	PowerPoint
MAPPING:	Prophet Dawud (as), Prophet Sulayman (as)	TIMELINING:	Prophet Dawud (as), Prophet Sulayman (as)

SKILL:

This week, we will focus on step 1 through 3. Read the text (step 1), and think about the main points of the text (step 2).
Ask yourself the questions (**what, who, when, where, why and how**) and then re-read the text and actively make notes on the main points and difficult parts (Step 3). Make a summary of the main ideas in one or two sentences.

PROJECT:

You have already researched your topic for this week, so write a quick outline about the main events. Think of a catchy title and a topic sentence.
Pick a template to use for your presentation this week.
Add at least one image or clip art to your presentation that supports the main point.
Create a PPT with a minimum of **7 slides:** one introduction slide, 5 main point slides (one main point per slide) and one conclusion slide. pay attention to the colors you use.

WEEK: 18	PHOENICIANS		
KEYWORDS:	Phoenicians, Carthage	RESOURCES:	UILE
SKILL:	Summarizing	PROJECT:	Poster
MAPPING:	Phoenicia	TIMELINING:	Phoenicia

SKILL:

This week, we will focus on step 1 through 3. Read the text (step 1), and think about the main points of the text (step 2).
Ask yourself the questions (**what, who, when, where, why and how**) and then re-read the text and actively make notes on the main points and difficult parts (Step 3).Make a summary of the main ideas in **one paragraph.**

PROJECT:

Create your poster for this week. This week, pay special attention to color. Look at the colors in your image/graphic used, and match or complement them. Change the colors in your template. Create three different versions with different colors. Which one works best with the topic of this week?

Requirements: Pick a pre-made template based upon the parts of the poster needed. Add/remove parts as necessary. Title and subtitle should be correct. Image/graphics should match the topic. Whitespace should be used correctly. Colors should be changed: a minimum of three versions with different colors.

WEEK: 19	ASSYRIANS & PROPHET YUNUS (AS)		
KEYWORDS:	Assyrians, Babylon, Nineveh, Prophet Yunus (as)	**RESOURCES:**	UILE HI Super Servants Series
SKILL:	Summarizing	**PROJECT:**	Diagramming
MAPPING:	Prophet Yunus (as)	**TIMELINING:**	Assyria, Prophet Yunus (as)

SKILL:

This week, we will focus on all steps. Read the text (step 1), and think about the main points of the text (step 2).

Ask yourself the questions (**what, who, when, where, why and how**) and then re-read the text and actively make notes on the main points and difficult parts.

Read the text again (step 3), this time jotting down notes. Look at your notes: what are the main points? (step 4)

Make a summary of the main ideas in **one paragraph** (step 5).

PROJECT:

Diagram the events of the journey Prophet Yunus (as).

Use the the image on the this page to choose a diagram and use 5 steps above to guide you in making your diagram.

WEEK: 20	BABYLONIANS		
KEYWORDS:	Babylon, Nebuchadnezzar Prophet Uzair (as)	RESOURCES:	UILE
SKILL:	Summarizing	PROJECT:	Poster
MAPPING:	Babylon	TIMELINING:	Babylon

SKILL:

This week, we will focus on all steps. Read the text (step 1), and think about the main points of the text (step 2).

Ask yourself the questions (**what, who, when, where, why and how**) and then re-read the text and actively make notes on the main points and difficult parts.

Read the text again (step 3), this time jotting down notes. Look at your notes: what are the main points? (step 4)

Make a summary of the main ideas in **one paragraph** (step 5).

PROJECT:

Create your poster for this week. This week, pay special attention to color. Look at the colors in your image/graphic used, and match or complement them. Change the colors in your template. Create three different versions with different colors. Which one works best with the topic of this week?

Requirements: Pick a pre-made template based upon the parts of the poster needed. Add/remove parts as necessary. Title and subtitle should be correct. Image/graphics should match the topic. Whitespace should be used correctly. Colors should be changed: a minimum of three versions with different colors.

WEEK: 21	PERSIANS & GREEKS		
KEYWORDS:	Persia, Persepolis. King Darius, Media, Athens, Sparta	**RESOURCES:**	UILE
SKILL:	Summarizing	**PROJECT:**	Diagramming
MAPPING:	Persia, Greece	**TIMELINING:**	Persia, Greece

SKILL:

This week, we will focus on all steps. Read the text (step 1), and think about the main points of the text (step 2).
Ask yourself the questions (**what, who, when, where, why and how**) and then re-read the text and actively make notes on the main points and difficult parts.
Read the text again (step 3), this time jotting down notes. Look at your notes: what are the main points? (step 4)
Make a summary of the main ideas in **one paragraph** (step 5).

PROJECT:

Diagram the culture of Persia. The Persian culture was very unique in many ways: from the inventions like the Royal Road, Palace of Persepolis and more. Use the image on the this page to choose a diagram and use 5 steps above to guide you in making your diagram.

WEEK: 22	**GREECE**		
KEYWORDS:	Greece, Athens, Sparta, Alexander the Great	**RESOURCES:**	UILE
SKILL:	Mind Map	**PROJECT:**	Diagramming
MAPPING:	Greece	**TIMELINING:**	Greece

SKILL:

As you read, use sticky notes to make clusters of important points. Think of a name for each cluster.
- Sketch the central idea and the main branches.
- Use key words on each branch
- Use colors.

PROJECT:

This week, make a Venn Diagram (see the circled diagram below) to show the differences and similarities between Athens and Sparta. Each circle is one item, in this case each city gets its own circle. In the circles you write the differences between the cities. Where they overlap, you write the similarities.

Use the 5 steps above to guide you in making your diagram.

WEEK: 23	**CHINA**		
KEYWORDS:	Yellow River, Shang Dynasty, Zhou, Qin Dynasty, Han Dynasty	**RESOURCES:**	UILE
SKILL:	Mind Map	**PROJECT:**	Mind Map
MAPPING:	Ancient China	**TIMELINING:**	Ancient China

SKILL & PROJECT:

As you read, use sticky notes to make clusters of important points. Think of a name for each cluster.

- Sketch the central idea and the main branches.
- **Add on a level of sub-branches with sub-topics.**
- Use key words on each branch
- Use colors.

WEEK: 24   **AFRICA**

KEYWORDS: People of Nok,   **RESOURCES:**   UILE
Kingdom of Kush,
Kingdom of Axum

SKILL: Mind Map   **PROJECT:**   Mind Map

MAPPING: Africa   **TIMELINING:**   Africa

SKILL & PROJECT:

As you read, use sticky notes to make clusters of important points. Think of a name for each cluster.

- Sketch the central idea and the main branches.
- Add on level of sub-branches with sub-topics.
- Use key words on each branch
- Use colors.
- **Add images.**

WEEK: 25	INDIA		
KEYWORDS:	Aryan people, Mauryan Empire, Gupta Empire, Caste System, Buddhism	RESOURCES:	UILE
SKILL:	Mind Map	PROJECT:	Mind Map
MAPPING:	India	TIMELINING:	India

SKILL & PROJECT:

As you read, use sticky notes to make clusters of important points. Think of a name for each cluster.

- Sketch the central idea and the main branches.
- Add on level of sub-branches with sub-topics.
- Use key words on each branch
- Use colors.
- Add images.

WEEK: 26	**ARABIA**		
KEYWORDS:	Sabaa kingdom, Nabataea kingdom, Petra	**RESOURCES:**	UILE HI
SKILL:	Mind Map	**PROJECT:**	Mind Map
MAPPING:	Arabia	**TIMELINING:**	Arabia

SKILL & PROJECT:

As you read, use sticky notes to make clusters of important points. Think of a name for each cluster.

- Sketch the central idea and the main branches.
- Add on level of sub-branches with sub-topics.
- Use key words on each branch
- Use colors.
- Add images.

WEEK: 27	NATIVE AMERICANS		
KEYWORDS:	Adena, Hopewell, Maya, Olmecs, Nazca	**RESOURCES:**	UILE
SKILL:	Mind Map	**PROJECT:**	Mind Map
MAPPING:	America	**TIMELINING:**	America

SKILL & PROJECT:

As you read, use sticky notes to make clusters of important points. Think of a name for each cluster.

- Sketch the central idea and the main branches.
- Add on level of sub-branches with sub-topics.
- Use key words on each branch
- Use colors.
- Add images.

Take your time to truly make your mind map colorful and full with images and symbols

WEEK: 28	CELTS		
KEYWORDS:	Gaul, Britain, Ireland	RESOURCES:	UILE
SKILL:	Mind Map	PROJECT:	Mind Map
MAPPING:	Celts	TIMELINING:	Celts

SKILL & PROJECT:

As you read, use sticky notes to make clusters of important points. Think of a name for each cluster.

- Sketch the central idea and the main branches.
- Add on level of sub-branches with sub-topics.
- Use key words on each branch
- Use colors.
- Add images.

Take your time to truly make your mind map colorful and full with images and symbols

WEEK: 29   **ROME**

KEYWORDS: Romulus, Senate,   **RESOURCES:**   UILE
Punic Wars, Julius
Ceasar, Aqueducts

SKILL: Choice   **PROJECT:**   Diagramming

MAPPING: Roman Empire   **TIMELINING:**   Romans

SKILL:

We have practiced several skills throughout the year. Today, pick the one that you liked the best and use it to write down the information you have researched.

PROJECT:

Diagram the three time periods of the Romans. Make sure you choose a diagram that allows you to list the three periods, with space to write details for each.

Remember the 5 steps above to guide you in making your diagram. Use the image on the other page to help you choose.

WEEK: 30	PROPHET ZACHARIAH (AS) & PROPHET 'ESA (AS)		
KEYWORDS:	Bethlehem, Nazareth, Jerusalem, Prophet Zachariah (as), Prophet Yahya (as), Prophet 'Esa (as)	RESOURCES:	HI
SKILL:	Choice	PROJECT:	Choice
MAPPING:	Prophet 'Esa (as)	TIMELINING:	Prophet 'Esa (as)

SKILL:

We have practiced several skills throughout the year. Today, pick the one that you liked the best and use it to write down the information you have researched.

PROJECT:

So far, we have covered how to create posters, how to put information in diagrams, how to produce good PowerPoint presentations, and how to make beautiful mind maps. We are sure you have a preference, so pick one of these methods to create something visually stunning.

RUBRICS & CHECK-LISTS

A Word on Scoring

When evaluating a project, each of the evaluation categories (Excellent, At Level, Needs Work, and Insufficient) is assigned a point. Excellent gets 4 points, At Level gets 3, Needs Work gets 2 and Insufficient gets 1 point. At the bottom of each Rubrics, the total amount of points is mentioned. Add up all the points a student scored in each category and divide by the total number of points. Then multiply with 100 to get the scored percentage.

For example: For diagramming a student scored the following:

Information: At Level: 3 points
Diagram: Needs Work: 2 points
Colors: Excellent: 4 points
Mechanics & Labeling: Excellent: 4 points

Total points scored: 3 + 2 + 4 + 4 = 13 points.
Total points possible: 16 points

The score of the student: 13/16 * 100 = 81%

RUBRICS

Rubric Poster

	Excellent	At Level	Needs Work	Insufficient
The Title & Subtitle	Topic and title clear and easily identified. Main idea is clearly appropriate to topic.	Topic and title are mostly clear and easily identified Main idea is appropriate to topic	Topic and title difficult to identify Main idea not clearly stated	Topic and title are not clearly identified No main idea
Graphics	All illustrations complement purpose of visual All Illustrations are of the same theme/color All illustrations are of high quality	Most illustrations complement purpose of visual Most Illustrations are of the same theme/color Most illustrations are of high quality	Few illustrations complement purpose of visual Few Illustrations are of the same theme/color Few illustrations are of high quality	Illustrations do not complement purpose of visual Illustrations are of different theme/color Illustrations are of low quality
Lay-out & White Space	Outstanding use of design and space Original and creative design Overall design is pleasing and harmonious	Adequate use of design and space Design is adequate Overall design is mostly pleasing and harmonious	Inappropriate use of design and space Design lacks creativity Lack of harmonious design in presentation	Little attempt to use design and space appropriately Design is dull Project has sloppy appearance
Colors	Outstanding use of color, Colors are complementary Colors are used to highlight important points	Adequate use of color Colors are complementary Color do not highlight important points	Inappropriate use of color Colors are low-contrast Colors highlight important points	Little attempt to use color Colors are low contrast and make reading difficult. Colors are not used to highlight important points

Total Points Possible: 16

Rubric Diagramming

	Excellent	At Level	Needs Work	Insufficient
Information	The problem is clearly presented in the diagram: within one glance the problem becomes clear	The problem is adequately presented in the diagram	The problem is unclearly presented in the diagram: only with verbal explanation does the problem become clear	The problem is not at all presented in the diagram
Diagram	The diagram chosen reflects the problem and the relationship of its components	The diagram chosen reflects the problem but not clearly the relationship of its components	The diagram chosen reflects the problem but not the relationship of its components	The diagram chosen does not reflect the problem
Colors	Several complementary colors are used to highlight the elements of the diagram	Several colors are used but they are not complementary Colors are used to highlight the elements of the diagram	Few colors are used but they are not complementary Colors are not used to highlight the elements of the diagram	No colors are used
Mechanics & Labeling	The diagram is labeled correctly The elements are labeled as well.	The diagram is labeled correctly But the elements are not labeled.	The diagram is not labeled correctly	The diagram is not labeled

Total Points Possible: 16

Rubric PowerPoint

	Excellent	At Level	Needs Work	Insufficient
Quantity	More than 7 slides Intro and conclusion slides present	Slides are adequate to present topic Intro and conclusion slides present	Slides sufficient to present topic No intro and conclusion slides present	Too little slides to present topic No intro and conclusion slides present
Template	Template lay-out is suitable for the topic Title is catchy Colors are adjusted	Template lay-out is suitable for the topic Title is present but not catchy Colors are adjusted	Template lay-out is not suitable for the topic or colors are not adjusted Or fields are left blank (if made online)	No lay-out templates used
Graphs	Graphs are two or more and are informative Colors are aligned to the design	Graphs are informative, but very few Colors are not aligned to the design	Graphs are used but not informative	No graphs used
Slide Design	One main point per slide Colors are supportive of the topic	One main point per slide Colors are not supportive of the topic or distract	Too much information per slide	Too much or no info on the slides
Graphics & Images	Support the main topic All illustrations are aligned to each other	Support the main topic Illustrations are not aligned to each other	Do not support the main topic	No graphics or images used

Total Points Possible: 20

Rubric Mind Map

	Excellent	At Level	Needs Work	Insufficient
Preparation	One main idea per sticky note Grouped into clusters	Too much info on sticky notes Grouped into clusters	Used sticky notes Not grouped into clusters	Did not use sticky notes
Central Idea	One clear central idea that clearly relates to the topic	One clear central idea that does not clearly relates to the topic	One central idea but did not relate to topic	No central idea
Branches	Uses main branches and several sub branches. Uses tertiary branches	Uses main branches and several sub branches.	Uses main branches and no sub branches	No main branches
Keywords/Links	Use keywords on the main branches and the subbranches. Uses links between different subbranches	Use keywords on the main branches and the subbranches.	Uses keywords on the main branches only	Uses no keywords
Colors & Graphics	Uses colors for each main branch and its subbranches Uses images/drawings	Uses colors for each main branch and its subbranches	Uses colors for each main branch	Does not use colors or images

Total Points Possible: 20

CHECK-LISTS

Check-list Outlining

Uses one main point per line

Uses Roman Numerals

Uses on phrase per Roman Numeral

Uses secondary points

Uses lower case letters for secondary points

Check-list Note Taking

Writes definitions

Uses own words

Uses number list and/or bullet points

Uses abbreviations

Check-list Summarizing

Uses own words

Reduces every paragraph to one or two sentences